What is astral projection

Why learn astral projection? 21

Models and theories of astral travel explained..........29

Mystical model..29

Phasing model..31

Different types of Astral Projection 35

Standard Astral Projection.............................35

Etheric Projection 36

Virtual reality projection 38

Remote Viewing vs. Astral Projection.........39

FAQs about astral projection 45

What does astral travel feel like?................45

What happens to the body during projection? 46

What does it feel like when you are actually out of your body?..47

The most common beginner mistakes and obstacles .. 53

1: Self-Doubt...53

2: Not breathing the right way....................54

3: Panicking..55

Astral projection side effects **59**

How To Astral Project: A Step-By-Step Guide (Multiple techniques) **67**

Preparation 67

When to actually do these techniques 69

1: The Rope Technique 70

2: The Hammock Technique 74

3: The Ladder Technique 76

4: The Point Shift Method 76

5: The sleep watching method 79

6: The Monroe Technique 82

7: Displaced-awareness technique 84

8: The Jump Technique 86

9: Muldoons Thirst Technique 87

10: The Stretch Out Technique 89

11: Finding objects or information 90

12: The lucid dreaming method 91

13: The Self-Visualization Method 92

14: The Rolling-Out Technique for Projection 96

15: The Kick System 97

16: The Picture Technique..99

17: The "Stay awake" method 100

Tips and Tricks for Success 105

What is the best time to project? 112

Wake up, Get up, and go back to bed tip..................113

How is the pineal gland linked? 114

Activation of the Pineal Gland...................................116

Final thoughts 121

Bonuses and resources...122

What is astral projection?

What is astral projection?

Here's the official definition:

Astral travel refers to an intentional out-of-body-experience (OBE) that allows one to travel the astral plane in a different mode of consciousness.

It is a separation from the physical body that allows a person to spiritually travel throughout the universe in order to explore a different level of spiritual awareness than is normally possible in day-to-day life.

It has primarily been described by those who have dedicated their lives to spiritual and mystical endeavors even though children demonstrate a natural ability to do astral travel.

But where did it come from?

Who discovered it, and why?

Well, Astral projection is not a modern spiritual practice.

It has been known throughout history for a very long time. Astral projection has been practiced for thousands of years, and the first recorded astral projections were in China. In all likelihood, people were practicing this form of travel long before that though.

Many traditional texts mention shamans who were people who were able to travel through time and space with astral projection. They are people who have trained to overcome the common mindset of space-time conditioning.

Shamans were able to move around in space, and can go far and come back in just a moment.

According to shamans, astral projection is one of the most enduring features of the mystical tradition underlying most of the major religions (The concept of becoming separated from yourself is widespread throughout many religions, sometimes called meditation, reflections etc).

Essentially, astral projection has been included and involved with most major religions throughout history. It's also been used by cultures that don't or didn't identify with a specific religion.

What's really interesting about it, is that astral projection has endured most of history. Throughout various wars, revolutions and changes astral projection has always been practiced and known, throughout it all.

In fact it's said that most 'super civilisations' like Ancient Egypt for example, used astral projection to gain knowledge of things that were FAR ahead of their time.

The knowledge of electrical power, for example, which would have been incredibly difficult to discover back then. It leads you to ask he question 'how DID they get that sort of information?'.

For many generations after the first written accounts of astral travel, it was slightly less discussed—primarily due to religious Puritanism and censorship.

However, the idea of astral travel has regained some popularity in recent years, especially in the Western world.

While widely associated with the 'New Age' movement, there are reports of practitioners across many spiritual and religious traditions. It doesn't seem to be linked to any ONE type of person or religion.

What is the experience of astral actually travel like?

Describing and/or defining it is near impossible because of the wide variety of experiences. Certainly astral experiences are influenced by a person's religious and cultural heritage. However, there tends to be some common threads that run through what people report—no matter their background.

The traveler may find himself in unfamiliar territory that is usually analogous to one's spiritual state. What this really means, is that you'll have the experience that reflects your mental and emotional state. If you're angry or depressed when you astral travel, you'll have a bad experience.

If however you're happy and motivated when you start you'll have a much better and more productive experience. For this reason, you have to make sure that your mindset is right before you attempt to have an OBE.

We'll cover some techniques and exercises for doing that later, but just bear it in mind for now.

In the astral realm, the normal laws of physics don't really apply. For instance, you may suddenly be able to float or fly in a new dimension.

What one sees depends on one's own state of mind at the time of travel. An astral environment may be cheerful and vivid if that is the current state of the astral traveler or it may be dull and depressing if that is the corresponding mindset of the traveler.

An astral plane may be calming and beautiful, or it may look dull or frightening to the traveler. Because what we see corresponds to our own spiritual state, it is important to set out on this endeavor spiritually grounded.

Some people who practice astral travel also report an ability to access the Akashic Records which are records of all human experiences that have ever occurred—thoughts, feelings, words, intentions and consciousness.

These records are probably one of the most impressive and mind blowing things to experience in an OBE. For beginners, they're quite hard to access, but if you keep practicing you'll be able to access them at will.

Because of the enormity of this prospect, proper intention is essential.

The validity of astral projection is widely debated because it is such a subjective experience. It's hard to say something is or isn't real when the only person that can really experience it is you.

It can't be tracked, recorded or monitored by anyone else. It's not like you can step on a treadmill and have people WITNESS you running, because it's all in your mind and in a realm that we can't perceive with our normal senses.

However, people across all sorts of religious and spiritual traditions have reported the ability to separate from the physical body and their stories reflect remarkable similarities. What's really interesting is how similar these thousands of stories all are. They vary slightly but the core IDEA and descriptions of astral projection remain the same.

Why would SO many people lie about it? It wouldn't benefit them in any way.. It's just like near death experiences.. What motivation would those millions of people have to make something like that up?

Although we now DO have scientific evidence to show that brain activity continues for a period of time after death, and that all sections of the brain light up like a Christmas tree.

MASSIVE neural activity happens in the minutes following death, and this makes perfect sense.

When you consider the descriptions of seeing a brilliant white light, rising from the body, seeing your past memories and lives, and being completely at peace. It makes sense then, that the brain activity of someone experiencing all of that would be off the charts.

The problem is, we just haven't found a good enough way of testing astral projection. But don't worry, science is advancing all the time and there will be evidence to support it within a few years.

Also, consider the nature of science, and of studies. Who actually FUNDS the studies that get done?

Well, it's usually big companies with something to sell.

Scientific studies and tests are VERY expensive to run. So it's VERY unlikely that one would be run that didn't benefit a company in some way. Often meat or dairy companies run studies to try and show that their food products are healthy, when they're really not.

In the past, tobacco companies have run studies in attempts to show that their brand of tobacco isn't AS BAD as some others. They pump LOTS of money into studies that are designed in a way to show them in a good light.

But why would any company spend a huge amount of money to prove that astral projection is real? How would it make them any money?

And it's not like there's a charity focused on learning more about astral projection either so we're sort of stuck for now.

While there is no scientific evidence in support of being able to leave the body, many people are deep believers. There are millions of personal testimonials and stories from people who REALLY know they've had this experience.

Most often, astral travel is practiced in conjunction with lucid dreaming and different forms of meditation. Through leaving the physical body, it is possible to hover above one's environment and observe one's surroundings from a different perspective. By doing this practice with intention, you can pursue spiritual questions that you set before traveling.

Those who practice astral projection say that they are aware of their change in consciousness as it is happening and that the sensory experience is quite different from the experience of their normal day-to-day lives. A traditional sense of time does not exist on the astral plane and there also isn't a typical sense of spatial dimension while traveling.

All of this can be discombobulating and confusing in the beginning; however, those who do astral projection say that it becomes more normal over time. After the experience is over, travelers report that they are able to vividly recall what they experienced while they were in another dimension.

Mystics say that the dreaming mind is where the spirit resides and a clue that one is on the right path to astral travel is that the frequency of having flying of falling dreams or dreams that end with waking up with a jerk become more common.

Some have even theorized that dreams are really a journey to the astral realm. In fact, it's been said that lucid dreaming is the first step towards astral projection and involves much of the same types of exercises.

Also dream yoga, an advanced form of lucid dreaming can also be linked to astral projection, and often if you learn one, you also know how to do the other.

The universe is thought to be divided into planes that vary in vibrational frequency. Where we typically think of humans living is considered the lowest vibrational frequency. As one evolves spiritually, one moves through the different planes to a higher vibrational level.

Many report that there are seven levels of human existence and that our mission as human beings is to develop and travel through all of them.

The astral realm is thought to only be a small part of all that is in the universe. Imagination and creativity play a huge role in how one experiences the astral realm, as well as other realms.

Imaginative people have more vivid experiences in the astral realm, because what happens in our mind influences the outcome.

Astral dwellers are commonly reported from travelers. Many are deceased loved ones but some souls that are seen are not known to the traveler. Some have important messages for the traveler and others pass by in more dream like state. Some are said to be working out their karma in order to accomplish what they could not accomplish in their earthly lifetime.

There are said to be three highest planes of the astral realm. They begin at the theological level and then move into the philosophical level—finally transcending both in the plane of joyful creativity and expression. As astral beings move up the continuum, they improve their given talents and abilities and continue to develop.

You might be wondering how easily this experience actually is to have. Some people can spontaneously project from childhood, because this is when we are most open to our natural abilities. It's also when we have fewer culturally imposed limits and restrictions about mystical endeavors.

Unfortunately, many have had it in ingrained in them that this practice only opens people up to negative forces and consequently some are too fearful to learn to do it. However, if a person has an open mind and spirit for the experience, in all likelihood, it will be possible to eventually learn to do it with practice.

Why learn astral projection?

Why learn astral projection?

Before we go on, here are some quick and powerful reasons to WANT to learn astral projection. There are of course LOTS more reasons, but these are just some of the main ones:

1. Learn to fly and soar over mountains! Just like in lucid dreaming but more powerful!

2. Past life glimpses: See what your relatives and YOU were doing in your past life/lives

3. Confirm life purpose, and finally know why you're here. It's said that each of us has a unique and divine life purpose. It's often hard to find but through astral travel you can unlock it

4. Education: Learn things, practice things, and improve! You can visit the divine records, or learn things from people throughout history

5. More joy in life, and more joy that you can give to those you love

6. Healing: Heal emotional damage or improve your self esteem, and then take that improved confidence back to the real world

7. Spirituality: Learning more about the spiritual world and what it all means, as well as

understanding different points of view and knowing what it's like to BE someone else

8. Meet your guides: It's said that we all have 'dream guides' or astral guidance who can help you through life tough moments and help you make decisions

9. Confirm life after death: Many astral travels report being able to see in clear detail what happens after death although this is not for beginners and may take some time to experience

10. Develop psychic abilities: You can learn through astral projection to hone your psychic abilities including telepathy, mind reading and seeing into the short term future. This takes lots of practice though, and we won't cover this depth in the beginners guide

These benefits are not ALL of them either.

There are plenty of benefits, but to be honest most people just want to SEE what it's like! They just want to experience this new reality, this new way of seeing the world. Because most of us aren't told about this stuff, and we can't learn it at school.

So when you first hear about something like astral projection, your first reaction is 'I WANT TO DO IT

NOW!'. And that's great, that desire and motivation will help you learn.

But bear in mind that although it's really exciting, it will take a few weeks to master. You can't instantly have an OBE sadly. Although, you may get lucky and if you're the right sort of person, you might be able to have an astral projection experience on your first night!

But it's important to set realistic goals ad expectations, so give yourself a month.

Say for the next 30 days, I'm going to practice these techniques and give it my best shot. Practice every day and become obsessed about this, and you'll have the best chance of doing it.

Probably one of the most profound benefits is being able to verify our immortality. Being able to EXPERIENCE something outside of your physical body is a huge thing. This means life as you know it can continue even after you're dead.

This also means that you will carry on living through your astral body, and for many people this is life changing. How differently would live if you KNEW that you could never truly die? If you knew that you could always continue in another body or even another universe or realm.

That's a life changing realisation for many people and one that shouldn't be taken lightly. Many people go into a deep state of meditation and reflection when they first realise this. When they realise that they are immortal.

It's not just in the next life that astral projection is awesome though. You'll experience much more restorative and relaxing sleep by astral projecting. This happens for one or two nights after your astral projection experience too, so the effects linger for a while.

Another thing you'll notice, is that when you realise we're inter-dimensional beings capable of being immortal, everything's easier.

Your personal development, your life goals, ANYTHING you want to achieve in life is instantly easier and within your reach.

Life becomes like a game for you, and you see how far you can push it. You see how much you can achieve, and what you can DO with your life! You're suddenly alive, more than you've ever been before. This might happen the first time you astral project, or maybe the second but it's going to happen pretty quickly.

Your brain literally expands and becomes faster. By unlocking astral projection and flexing that 'muscle' for the first time in your life, you begin to unlock your true abilities. Your hidden talents, skills and things you were BORN to do. This is very exciting.

There are other benefits too, but for most people it's pretty intense.

It's hard to take all of this in, especially if you've never experienced astral travel before. For beginners this whole process can be overwhelming, so slow down. Take this one step at a time and learn the techniques fro the ground up.

Models and theories of astral travel

Models and theories of astral travel explained

Astral projection is one of those terms that means different things to different people.

Before we can get into the techniques to actually do it, I feel it's important to look at the theories and models of WHY and HOW we can astral project.

The term "astral" has sometimes functioned as a "catch all" term. However, there are really some finer levels of differentiation to be explored that will be covered in this section.

There are actually various types of astral projection and travel. It's not just ONE thing and it's not even just one PLACE that we're able to travel to. There are several layers, levels and realms that we can learn to travel to and experience.

Mystical model

The mystical model of astral projection encompasses many belief systems, but the facet that ties them all together is that projection happens OUTSIDE the physical body.

A different body, one that is more subtle and comprised of energy exists outside the physical body. The more subtle body is connected to the physical body energetically and is connected together by a cord that connects the chakras into the more subtle form of consciousness.

This is known as the silver cord.

You might have heard this mentioned in various articles about astral projection, but essentially it works like this:

The silver cord is a long thin string like energy that connects your astral body to your physical one. This ensures you never get separated or lost, and you can always find your way instantly back to your physical body.

To be honest, you won't need to use it or even be aware of it most of the time. In most cases simply thinking or intending to arrive back at your physical body is more than enough.

You'll be sent hurtling back to your real world body in no time. but it's useful to know it's there, and it acts as peace of mind if nothing else.

Phasing model

Defined by Dr. Robert Monroe, the phasing model, is the belief that it ISN'T possible to leave the body physically, but that the astral world and the physical world are different points on the consciousness continuum.

When a person travels astrally, they enter into another form of consciousness.

One of the clues that one has exited physical reality is the state of the mind being awake but the body being asleep which lends itself to the idea that perhaps external reality is an internally created state.

This model is probably the most interesting, as it sounds easy to imagine. Imagine your consciousness like a scale or spectrum. When we're awake, we're experiencing one part of the spectrum, and when we're asleep, another.

when we dream we experience another part, and then when we LUCID dream, we experience a more aware state.

Then imagine that when we astral project, we're simply experiencing another state of consciousness.

To be honest, it doesn't matter which model you believe in, if any. The fact is if you practice the techniques we'll cover shortly, you will have these experiences.

And then once you've ACTUALLY had the experience of an OBE, you can make your own mind up about how it works. You can decide which model or theory you want to believe in and come to your own understanding of how it works.

You don't really NEED to know how it works if you don't want to though! It's like dreams.. Most of us have no idea how dreams work, or how the brain is able to create such intense and vivid dream scenes but we don't really care.

We just enjoy the experience and learn what it has to offer us. If you're familiar with lucid dreaming, the chances are you know HOW to have a lucid dream but you don't really understand the neural science and how the brain actually FUNCTIONS during a lucid dream. This is much the same. You can learn the science if you want, but for the most part, people are just interested in having the experience and the benefits it can bring them.

Types of astral projection

Different types of Astral Projection

Standard Astral Projection

In standard astral projection, the traveler arrives in a domain that feels real which, as stated before, usually reflects one's own inner reality.

Environments are widely varying and can be both positive or negative for the traveler. Projectors May see the past or the future and may also have access to the Akashic records.

This is probably where 80% of astral travels find themselves. In an astral realm much like a lucid dream, in which they can move around and choose what to do. They're connected to the physical body by a silver cord, and with practice they can remember the things they've done in the OBE.

Most people at first CAN'T remember things they've done, and instead just return to their bodies knowing that SOMETHING profound has happened. But they're unable to describe exactly WHAT has happened. It's something that you can improve and work on with practice though, much like remembering your normal dreams.

Etheric Projection

Etheric projection is when the out-of-body experience involves moving about in ghost-like form in PHYSICAL reality.

However, this world may have some differences from regular physical reality if mind control is not maintained.

This is sometimes called Real Time Projection (RTP) and the physical world as we typically understand it is called the "Real Time Zone", or "RTZ." From the Real Time Zone, travelers are able to access the astral plane, OR remain in the RTZ and be an onlooker for Real Time events.

This is often confused with astral travel. Etheric travel is primarily associated with the physical world. The etheric double is a medium between the astral and physical realms. Ether is the "vital force" that propels the physical body to experience this different form of consciousness.

So, it's in THIS realm that people are able to do things like see information in other rooms, visit their friends in other parts of the physical world, or send 'messages' to people.

A common experiment that was done in this realm showed somebody projecting across a state to 'see' their friend and then returned to the physical world to tell them what they were doing or something similar.

It's a difficult experience to have and this is probably the most difficult thing to learn. Because it's linked with the physical world, the experiences here are much more fragile.

The physical world is often very disconnected from the astral realm. It makes interacting in the REAL world difficult because they're so different.

Often people get this state confused with astral projection. People assume that just because they can't astral project and 'see inside their friends kitchen' it's all fake and doesn't work.

That's not the case! They're just trying to perform one of the most difficult feats in astral projection, even for experts!

For most of us, 'STANDARD' astral projection is the thing we're aiming for. This is the first step, and then when you've learned a bit more and you can reliably have OBEs, THEN move onto doing something like Etheric projection.

Virtual reality projection

Virtual Reality Projection is when a projector moves on the physical plane and interacts with the astral plane at the same time.

An example of this is the projector walking into a "real" photo and being transported to this place. This is a result of concentrated experience and a person steps into this reality from their own focus on changing consciousness.

Again, this is a very advanced form of astral projection, and most people never get close to this in their normal life. It takes years of practice and meditation, and even then not everyone can do it.

Being able to phase into physical reality so easily takes a lifetime of dedication. There have been those who have spent their lives doing this, but I wouldn't recommend this for most people. For most people, simply learning the standard astral projections techniques is more than enough.

Remote Viewing vs. Astral Projection

Remote Viewing refers to gathering information about a distant location using paranormal means or extra-sensory perception. Typically a remote viewer gives information about an object that is hidden from view, and is far away.

This is an interesting skill, because it's actually NOT astral projection at all. It's just using your natural abilities to percept something that's not in your reach normally.

An example would be your friend finds an image or draws an image on a bit of paper, without showing you. Then you close your eyes, and attempt to SEE the image in your MINDS eye.

This is not about guessing.

You're actually using your divine powers and universal consciousness to see the image inside THEIR mind. You can learn to do this in a few days actually. You'll find that in a relatively short period of time you can learn to see basic outlines and shapes, or things like whether it's outside or inside.

Most of us when we learn remote viewing, learn some basics techniques are we can get to a fairly good level of ability.

You'll be able to see details like whether there are curvy lines or straight lines.. Whether it's an animal or an object.. or the direction of the main LINES and shapes in the image.

These things when you actually percept them are VERY unlikely to be random.

Of all the images and shapes you could have imagined, you'll be able to see fairly accurately what the image actually is. It won't be a clear image in your head though. It will often be a glimpse of a black and white line or direction.

Sometimes it will just be a feeling or a word. You can then link that word or feeling to the image, and you'll find that it's scarily accurate.

But it's not astral projection. The confusion comes because by learning astral projection, you IMPROVE your natural abilities like remote viewing as well. It's sort of like a side effect. But we're not talking about remote viewing here, this is all about astral projection!

FAQ about astral projection

FAQs about astral projection

What does astral travel feel like?

Most say that astral projection is an experience that transcends words. However, there are some commonalities that practitioners have consistently described.

Astral projection is not the norm for most people, and it can feel scary at first when one is about to embark on such an unpredictable journey.

On the other hand, if one can learn to recognize some of the more classic predictors of an impending astral projection, one can be more prepared and therefore calmer about the experience.

Remember that these signs are a positive sign and indicative that an astral experience is near.

Many people get to the point of exiting the body and then get so frightened that they fail to do so. Being prepared and knowing the possible symptoms, makes it more likely that you will leave your body. Some people become convinced that they are going to die, and this naturally puts some people off to the point that they no longer want to project.

By being knowledgeable about the process, you will be more apt to be able to work through any difficulties that may arise, and success is more likely.

What happens to the body during projection?

Although it's largely unknown what happens to the body during astral projection, there have been a few theories.

The most common theory is that molecules and chemicals (DMT) and crystals (calcite) in the pineal gland are being compressed releasing photons.

The scientific name for this process is called "piezoluminescence." This process makes crystals in the pineal gland that reflect light and then that is interpreted by the brain in a variety of ways. But as we said, there's not much that is known for certain about the astral projection experience, and we're constantly learning new things every year. Hopefully one day we'll understand how it works!

What does it feel like when you are actually out of your body?

Once the exit has been made, there is feeling of being weightless and that one is floating.

All of the usual presumptions about movement are no longer valid. It won't be possible for you to move as you do in the earthly realm with your physical body because there are no body parts to receive commands for movement in the astral realm.

In this new realm, it will be necessary to learn to WILL the body to move in different ways. It's all about your intention as we'll cover later.

Here's a list of some of the sensations you may experience, so that you will be prepared for your journey:

1. **Rapid heart rate:** It's important to try to remain calm as your heart rate increases. Many people report rapid heart rate that feels as if one has just completed an intense cardio workout. Others report it as a jolt to the senses—as if one has been mildly shocked. If this happens, remind yourself that the sensation is only

temporary, and do your best to ride out the sensations without panicking.

2. **Vibrations:** This is perhaps the most common physical effect that people describe while doing astral projection. If this occurs, it is a positive sign that you are on your way to projection. Intensity varies from person to person. For some, the vibrations are minimal while others describe the experience as volcanic. Interestingly enough, if others are watching while one is exiting the body, it is reported that the spectators are not able to see any movement in the body of the traveler. This is indicative that the astral self is about to separate from the physical body.

3. **Paralysis and stiffness:** Sleep paralysis is sometimes reported during the process because one is in the hypnagogic state—which is when only the mind and not the body is active. When this happens, sleep paralysis is possible. If the fear becomes unmanageable during paralysis, it is possible to pull one's self out of this state. However, it's important to remember that this physical side effect can actually be helpful to the process.

4. **Numbness and tingling:** Some travelers become very sensitive to physical sensations when going through the process of separating from the body. This may become evident in a few different ways. The first possibility is experiencing tingling in all or part of the body. The intensity varies from person to person. Another possible sensation is itching with some people reporting that it is sometimes quite unbearable. Alternately, one may lose all sensation in the body.

5. **Sensation of pressure:** One may experience pressure sensations while preparing to exit the body. As with all of the other symptoms, try to be patient as you experience these sensations because they will inevitably pass. The most common part of the body that experiences pressure is the head (or crown chakra) because this is where energy exits the body.

6. **Heat sensations:** When the process begins, the naval chakra heats up and the heat rises throughout the body in order to prepare to exit. This is a natural physical reaction to energy building within the body in order to be released into the astral realm.

7. **Sounds:** Sounds are one of the more common symptoms experienced by travelers. Common noises that people report include buzzing, popping, roaring or a the sound of being in a wind tunnel. As with all of the other effects, try to maintain calm and focus through them and the symptoms will eventually pass.

Most common beginner mistakes

The most common beginner mistakes and obstacles

I thought it would be very useful to understand a few of the most common mistakes that beginners make. This way, you can set yourself up for success before your even START learning the techniques.

I think this is very important because a lot of people will read a guide like this and get very over excited. They'll want to just do everything instantly, without really understanding how it works or what the focus should be on. For that reason please don't skip this section.

1: Self-Doubt

You cannot achieve anything that you do not believe in.

You must really have faith that it is possible to astral project, and that the spirit realm is real. When you are lying on your bed with your eyes shut, block out all other thoughts.

The idea is to stare into the darkness without any other thought crossing your mind. This is how you will slowly reach the state where your mind is awake but your body is not.

Going into astral projection half-hearted means that you will not be able to give your all to the process making it difficult to get results.

I could write lots more on belief and intention, but let's leave it at that. The beliefs you hold will dictate what you're able to do, so if you WANT to astral project you must really start believing that you CAN.

2: Not breathing the right way

One of the things that you can easily control is your breathing. By regulating your breaths, you are more in tune with your body and you can send yourself to projection.

When your breathing isn't regulated, you will not be able to relax or concentrate enough. This will inhibit the astral projection process since this is one of the most important elements for projection.

Your breathing needs to be focused but not forced. You should focus on how your breathing feels, and be AWARE of it, but don't try and control it. Much of the meditation techniques you can learn involve focusing on your breathing, and for good reason.

Your breath is a divine way of connecting with true consciousness. We all breathe, all the time, but how often are you REALLY aware of your breath and how it feels?

It's important to take a few minutes every single day to really focus on your breathing. Focus on how fast or slow it is, and what it sounds like.

But don't try and change it or force a new way of breathing. The goal is to just be AWARE of how you currently breathe. That's it!

3: Panicking

Beginners have quite a few fears that make it difficult to achieve astral success. Fears are most common during separation. Feelings of anxiety, as well as shock that it is actually happening, may be enough to cause someone to pull back from projection.

Try not to panic about any of this. Even during some of the techniques when you experience sleep paralysis, try and remain as calm as possible, and not panic.

If you panic, you'll just scare yourself and bring yourself OUT of the astral projection experience.

There's really nothing to panic about because you KNOW what's going to happen. Sure it's going to be exciting and different when you first experience it, but there's nothing to be afraid of. As long as you focus on doing the techniques exactly as they're taught, you'll be fine.

With this sort of thing, it's important to meditate every day. Not only does this make your vibrations higher and make astral travel more likely, but it relaxes you and removes stress. By being less stressed about the whole thing, you're much more likely to be able to do it.

Also, one of the most common reasons beginners fail at lucid dreaming and astral projection is they wake themselves up too early because they panic. By panicking, you're just going to end your experience prematurely.

Side effects and dangers

Astral projection side effects

We're almost at the astral projection techniques, I promise!

I think it's important to have context and backstory before jumping into the techniques. This way you're more likely to understand and practice them, because you actually know how they work.

A common fear that people have about astral projection is that they will die during the process.

There is no known case of anyone dying while projecting. It is often said that a "silver cord" attaches the physical body to the astral body which has perpetuated the idea that one will die if the cord is severed.

That being said, it is always best to practice projection in a space that feels safe and protected, like your own bedroom, if for no other reason than a sense of psychological and spiritual safety.

Another common fear is the fear of possession while on the astral plane. In the first stages of astral projection, travelers end up on one of the lower planes, and this is where malevolent spirits are said to most often be hanging around.

While it's not clear if there is actual possession on the astral plane, it is nonetheless wise to protect one's self as much as possible along the way.

Some common protection techniques include the following methods: imagining a white protective light around yourself and calling on guides for protection.

It's important to remember that it is generally thought that it is necessary for an invitation for possession to happen in order for it to occur. Therefore, if one is clear in one's intention regarding astral travel, possession isn't likely.

By the same token, by sending your consciousness to the astral plane, you are establishing a connection with it.

This type of deep connection may bring some negative experiences into your life that may need to be worked through once you return to the earthly realm.

Once you have established that astral connection, it is possible that you will see unusual things that you have never seen before in both the earthly and astral realm. Grounding and protection techniques are the best way to ward these experiences off.

Some other side effects include obsession. I've mentioned that it's actually good to become obsessed about astral projection, at least at first. This is because I think for beginners, a LOT of effort and practice is needed to get to the point where you can actually do this.

And the only real way of getting there is to become temporarily obsessed with it, so you're motivated to actually get it done. Otherwise, you'll just forget about it and you'll never really learn how to do it.

It's really sad that lots of people start learning how to astral project, but then when they can't get the techniques to work, they give up! They forget about it, and in a few months time they might ask themselves why they even bothered starting!

If you actually put the work in, and practice these techniques every single day UNTIL they work, they will work. There's no way they cannot! Everyone has the potential and ability to project, but NOT everyone will put in the work to actually get there.

Hopefully if you're still reading this, you're one of the people who WILL put in the work and actually practice these things every day for at least two months. But it might take longer! If you haven't had an OBE by two months, keep going!

Why would you stop if you haven't actually astral projected yet?

One more danger I thought I should mention is astral exhaustion.

Some people can find that after astral projecting for the first time they enter the real world again with a profound and overwhelming sense of fatigue and exhaustion.

This doesn't affect everyone but it can be annoying and tiring.

Think of it like the pain you might feel if you lifted heavy weights for the first time in your entire life. Your muscles would be sore and you'd feel very tired and worn out, right? Imagine that sort of exhaustion but in your mind.

You've probably felt it before like when you've gone on a long flight and not been able to sleep, but you're really tired so your body is just craving the bed to be able to sleep?

Well, it's similar. Make sure that at least for the first time you astral project, you've not got much to do the next day. This way you can give your body the rest it will need afterwards.

But like I said, this doesn't happen to everyone, far from it. It's usually about 20% of first time projectors that get this astral exhaustion, but I thought I should mention it just in case, so you know what to prepare for.

If you DO get this happen to you, there are some simple ways of avoiding it or making it pass easier. Just firstly, go back to sleep!

If you've done this in the early hours of the morning, just go back to sleep for a few hours and then you should wake up peaceful and refreshed.

If you can't go back to sleep, try just laying down with your eyes closed, while listening to some relaxing music. It could also help to have a warm bath, which can help to soothe you. You'll find that the fatigue doesn't last more than a couple of hours anyway, but during those hours it can feel very overwhelming.

You certainly won't be able to focus on anything like reading and watching things if you do get this, but don't worry! It's usually the first 1-2 times people get this, and then it stops.

Once you've got yourself and your mind used to the experience, you actually end up feeling more refreshed and energetic after astral projecting anyway. And as I said, 80% of people don't get this, and just skip straight to the point where astral projection GIVES them energy!

So, we're about to cover the main techniques you can use to astral project and some tips and tricks for making it more likely, but before we do, just take a moment to get your mindset right. It's tempting to skip over a section like this and just jump straight in, but don't do that.

I know it's exciting and you just want to get started, but please take a few minutes to just think about it, and tell yourself you can do it. It makes all the difference.

Astral projection
TECHNIQUES

How To Astral Project: A Step-By-Step Guide (Multiple techniques)

Preparation

Before you try to do astral projection, it's important to make your space as comfortable as possible. Your space should be conducive to rest and relaxation.

While not essential, some helpful elements include the following items: plants, incense and candles. Also, try to make sure that nobody is going to come in and disturb you while attempting to project. Having an interruption is the fastest way to losing concentration during the projection process.

Focus is essential for success in projection. Some general tips include focusing on a particular body part, such as your foot. Be as still as possible and focus on the body part, until you can almost see every part of it in your mind.

There are many different techniques to get your soul out of body. One technique that works for some people may not work for others. Keep trying techniques until you find the one that works best for you.

Bear in mind that whichever technique you use, most people do not achieve results on the first attempt. It is easy to get frustrated but remember that with practice and effort over time you will see results.

Blockages are possible and it may take time to work through them. For examples, past traumas can be a hindrance and an unhealthy pineal gland can be a stumbling block, too.

Just one more time, remember that NOT every technique will work for you. That's why I've given you so many techniques here, because one of these WILL work. So don't give up if the first one doesn't work. Here's what you need to do:

Try each technique every night for two to four weeks. IF after weeks of trying that ONE technique nothing's happened, move onto the next one, and so on.

If you want to speed it up because you're impatient, you can but the results won't be as good. Make sure at the very least to give each

technique at least a week of trying it EVERY night!

When to actually do these techniques

This is an important note:

Most if not all of these techniques should be done in the early hours of the morning. This means you need to set your alarm for about 4-5AM and then wake up and do the techniques then.

You can of course do these WHENEVER you want, and they'll still work but your best chance of success is about 4-5AM.

Why?

Because your body and mind are in the perfect state for OBES during that time. Your body has just had 6 hours of deep restorative sleep, and your REM sleep periods are at their longest.

You've also got hormones like serotonin starting to enter your bloodstream to wake you up for the day, which makes your conscious brain more active.

There are a number of other scientific reasons, but take my word for it, this is the best time to do it. If you go to bed normally at about 10PM, aim to wake up at about 4-5AM to try these techniques.

1: The Rope Technique

This technique is probably the most well-known and popular method and it was first introduced by Robert Bruce. The technique uses visualization to achieve projection.

The first step for this technique is to of course wake up and make sure there's no light or sound in your bedroom. If the sun has already started to rise, that's fine but make sure there's no flashing LED lights or whirring sounds from any electronics.

Then lay down and close your eyes. Completely relax all of your muscles and really devote a few minutes to remain them. Make sure there's absolutely no tension in your body, including your jaw and neck.

Most people actually skip this part when learning the rope technique, but I promise you that's a mistake. The relaxation and preparation for this is probably the most important part!

By relaxing the body and mind you're much more likely to be able to do this, as this technique is all about visualisation.

After getting into a relaxed position, imagine a rope extending down from the ceiling.

Once the image is firmly in your mind, visualize reaching out with your hands and pulling yourself up the rope. You may experience feelings of dizziness or vertigo as you do this exercise and it usually intensifies as you progress up the rope.

As you continue to climb, you will begin to feel the vibrations and you may feel briefly paralyzed.

When this happens, it's important not to let the fear keep you from continuing. Be focused on climbing the rope and you will succeed. Eventually you will feel yourself exit the body and then you will be hovering above your body.

This will feel very strange at first, because the chances are you've never done this before. Don't let the experiences freak you out or panic you, just let them be. Just observe what is happening and how it feels.

Many people have found it helpful to pin or tape a length of ribbon or string to the ceiling above their beds or chairs, hanging within easy arm's reach.

Touch this occasionally until you get used to its position in your mind. The position and feel of the rope will grow in your awareness memory, making it easier to imagine yourself reaching out and climbing it with your awareness hands.

The important thing to remember about this technique is that you're using your visualisation of the rope to help you exit. It's all about how strongly you can picture that rope, and being able to IMAGINE your hand reaching out to grab it.

But of course it's not your real hand, it's your astral hand you're using. This is where most people get this wrong. They imagine moving their physical hand, and nothing happens.

Most guides on this technique online don't even mention this, but here's what you do:

Practice impinging moving your physical hand, right now. Imagine how your physical hand might feel to move and lift up above you. Now imagine instead moving an astral hand.

Because you've never done this before, it's hard to imagine what it might feel like, right? And so that's why most people just imagine lifting their real physical hand instead.

And that's where they go wrong.

So instead, picture this:

Imagine a see through, smooth and soft field of energy that looks a bit like your hand, but not completely. Imagine the feeling of moving, but you're not really feeling any muscles, bones or joints moving around.

It feels more like your hand passing through water.

Imagine the feeling of moving your hand around underwater, and in fact you can practice this in a waking life swimming pool. Just get used to the feeling and sensation of the hand, and your arm moving through the water.

That's the feeling you're going to imagine and visualise when doing the rope technique. Imagine the feeling of your astral hand (like water) moving up and grabbing the rope.

When you imagine your astral hand grabbing the rope, don't imagine diners or a physical solid 'grip'. Instead imagine the astral hand bonding with the rope, and sealing itself to it, like superglue. this might feel similar to the feeling you get when you put your hand on something really cold like a block of ice.

The feeling of the king sealing to the ice is what you're after, but this one I wouldn't suggest practicing in waking life. Imagine the feeling of sealing your hand to a block of ice or something really sticky like a bit of rope covered in superglue. That's the feeling you should visualise and imagine when grabbing the rope.

2: The Hammock Technique

This technique is a bit different than the rope technique but still uses the same visualisation methods. Imagine yourself in a hammock between two palm trees on a beach. Visualize the movements of the hammock, and feels the feelings of swaying in the hammock. Repeat until the vibrations occur, and then roll out of your body.

Now this doesn't need as much explanation as the rope technique because it's largely the same. Except instead of visualising the rope and imaging that you can reach it to pull you out, you're using a hammock.

If you've never actually been in a hammock, this might be hard to imagine. For those who have been in a hammock, you'll know the gentle swaying sensation you get if you're just laying there and there's a slightly gust of wind.

You can also create this effect by just gently swaying yourself back and forward and then stop moving completely.

That's the effect you're really after here, and it's a very subtle movement. Try and recreate this effect as you imagine the hammock and visualise it!

3: The Ladder Technique

Occasionally, people have difficulty with the rope technique for astral projection, as they just don't feel that their imaginary hands and arms are strong enough to hold them and pull them up the rope.

There's also the fact that ropes are fundamentally floppy and soft. It's sometimes hard to imagine pulling yourself up with such a thing, especially as the entire rope is in your mind and being imagined.

For that reason, you can try this:

A ladder may be imagined hanging from the ceiling instead which has the benefit of allowing the projector to use his or her feet in addition to the hands. All other aspects of this method remain the same as with the Rope Projection Technique.

4: The Point Shift Method

The next technique for Astral Projection is slightly more traditional and also more difficult for many people.

However, some people take to these kinds of astral projection techniques quite naturally, and it is certainly good to have as many different methods under your belt as possible.

The best place to be is where you know how to use various techniques, so you can decide which one to try on any given night.

Sure, it's good to practice each one on it's own for a while, but eventually you'll be at the point where you can choose a different technique each night and just go with what works best for you.

The point shift method involves becoming intensely aware of your own body, and then mapping out in your imagination where everything in your room is, in relation to you.

This technique actually involves etheric astral projection in a way, like we spoke about before. This is because you're going to be interacting a little bit with the physical realm. You're going to be projecting into the real world but into your own version of it, like a copy.

Imagine you're copying the layout of the bedroom you're in, and projecting into the copied version of it.

It is for this reason that it requires quite a lot of concentration.

So to get started, focus on thinking about your room and where everything is in it. Think about the distance between objects, the shapes, and the height of the bits of furniture.

Think about the details as well, like the materials things are made from and how it all feels. Remember this should all be done with your eyes closed, ideally in the dark.

Once this stage has been reached, you then can feel yourself float, just a few inches, at first, and then visualize all of your surroundings from that new perspective.

The idea is to feel as if you have already projected out of you body, and keeping your awareness of where you are and what you visualize from the viewpoint of your imaginary self!

Finally, you'll slowly rise from your physical body.

Again, this will feel strange. Also of all the techniques, this is the most likely to collapse and not last very long, because it's so close to physical reality.

That being said, if you can master this one, the other techniques will be a walk in the park for you! I think a lot of people tend to try and START with this technique, not realising it's one of the hardest ones to get results with.

This technique takes what can only be described as a very 'relaxed' form of will-power. Some force is necessary, but you must not allow your body to become tense.

5: The sleep watching method

This approach also requires getting into a comfortable position. Once you have settled into your surroundings, make sure that you are facing the ceiling by laying down on your back.

Spend time clearing your mind of extraneous thoughts and deepening your relaxation. You can meditate, or focus on tensing and then relaxing all your muscles in succession, whatever works best for you.

At this point, set your intention.

Tell yourself that you are going to watch yourself go to sleep as you let your body sleep but your mind will stay awake. The goal is to keep your consciousness while the body goes into the sleep state.

As you proceed, you will notice different sensations throughout your body. Heaviness and numbness is common and is a sign that you are on the right track. Other common physical sensations include the following possibilities: tingles, vibrations and buzzing.

These signal that an astral experience is close at hand.

Once you begin experiencing some or all of these experiences, begin to imagine that you are rising up toward the ceiling.

Spend time making this sensation last as long as possible. People often report that they find themselves outside their body at this point.

This is not to be confused with sleep paralysis.

Sleep paralysis will happen naturally during this technique, but that's not what you're aiming for. Sleep paralysis for those who don't know, is when your body paralyses your muscles while you're asleep.

So for this technique you will be asleep, or at least your body will be. And that's why you'll experience the onset of sleep paralysis. It's nothing to be scared of, it's just your body keeping you safe.

This way you can't act out your dreams and move around in the night, so it's a natural safety mechanism.

Annoyingly, the body also puts you into sleep paralysis when you're projecting, but it's ok. Just be aware of it and expect it to happen, that way it can't surprise you.

It feels like you're stuck to the chair or bed and you can't move. It can also feel like something is gently pressing down on your chest. Keep telling yourself while it happens that it won't hurt you, and that if you REALLY wanted to wake up or stop the experience, you can.

So like I said after a few minutes of sleep paralysis, you'll find yourself rising up slowly form your physical body. At first this awareness might be in black and white, or it might be very hard to notice what's happening.

For a lot of people at first, it's really hard to see ANYTHING during this process. As you practice it more and more, you'll be able to see your body more clearly. In fact I'd suggest leaving your light on a little bit for this technique so it's easier to see your body.

The absolute best conditions for this are to have the room lit by 2-3 candles around the corners of the room. The candle light should bounce off your body and let you see yourself as you rise up.

Also as you get more advanced, you can see in the dark while astral projecting anyway so you won't really need light, but that comes later.

6: The Monroe Technique

This method was first created by Dr. Robert Monroe, one of the foremost researchers on astral projection. As with all of the other methods, relaxation is key. Achieving the hypnagogic state, or the state between wakefulness and sleep, is critical.

After deepening your state of relaxation, try to induce vibrations and strengthen them as you progress. At some point, you will exit the body.

Another big part of this is to focus on a specific time that you're going to astral project. This helps you set your intention and your brain helps you get there.

By telling yourself in advance exactly when you plan on having an OBE, your brain helps you make that happen.

Much like in normal reality and waking life, if you set a clear goal, the universe helps you get it.

So, decide on a time that you want to have an OBE, and then commit to that. Let's say it's tomorrow morning at 430AM. Commit to that time and keep telling yourself that you'll astral project at that time.

Then you can use whatever technique you like during the set time!

7: Displaced-awareness technique

Close your eyes and move into a relaxed state. Try to perceive the entire room and particularly focus on your awareness from the shoulders.

Then visualize that your astral body shifts by 180 degrees. At this point, attempt rotate mentally so that your head is where your feet should be and vice versa. Once you achieve this, try visualizing your surroundings from your new perspective. Do this until projection takes place.

This is a really good one for beginners. Often it's hard to imagine something outside what we're used to, and this is a prime example of that. It's often hard to imagine moving around and looking at something that isn't in front of you.

By doing this, you make astral projection very likely! To clarify, you're not going to be physically moving at all. Just lay there in your bed, with your eyes closed. You can actually do this sitting down as well.

So you're sitting there in the chair, eyes closed, not moving at all. Now you imagine shifting your entire body around to see behind you, but all without moving your real body.

By doing this enough times, your astral body starts to dislodge from your physical one and you sort of fall out of your actual body. This will be awesome when you get it right because it happens so fast.

It feels like you've literally just fallen out of your body like it was a suit. Imagine doing this several times but try and sit down for this technique.

It's hard to imagine turning round from a laying down position so I think sitting is the easiest way of doing this one. I've had good success doing this while sitting down in a dimly lit room.

For this one, I like to have relaxing or ambient noises and sounds in the background. This helps set the scene and get me into the right frame of mind to astral project.

8: The Jump Technique

The Jump Technique is typically used to move into a lucid dream/OBE while sleeping. To prepare, it is recommended that people who desire to travel astrally ask themselves throughout the day if they are in a dream or not.

This helps a person ascertain if they are in a dream or in physical reality. In order to discern where we are in a dream, we jump to get the answer.

If you are still in the physical world, you will come back to the ground in the dream. If you have entered the astral realm, the jump will defy gravity and you will begin to float.

When this is done for a few days, you will soon find yourself in a dream in which you are jumping to check whether you are in a dream or not. As soon as you jump, you will find yourself floating, thus triggering a Lucid Dream and an OBE.

I should mention that this technique is much more for lucid dreaming than it is for astral projection. Although you can actually ENTER and OBE through a lucid dream, so it's entirely up to you if you practice this one or not.

Lucid dreams can be very similar to OBEs and you can have a great experience with both.

9: Muldoons Thirst Technique

This is not one of the most pleasant or fun methods, but it can be effective. To practice this technique, it's necessary to refrain from drinking liquids for a period of time before bed.

Leading up to the time you attempt to project, increase your level of thirst by any means possible.

It's helpful to even go as far as to set a glass of water in front of yourself, but not allowing yourself to drink from it.

Before bed, eat a bit of salt and then place the glass of water out of reach from your bed. Go over in your mind every necessary step to get to the glass of water. As you go to sleep, think about your thirst, but do not quench your thirst.

The purpose of this is to help facilitate waking up in the night still thinking about your thirst and walking toward the glass of water during sleep in the middle of the night. Although not considered to be one of the more effective methods, some people have reported success with this method.

Now bear in mind a few things about this, firstly it can be used along side other techniques. What you're doing is making your body crave the water that you know is on the other side of the room.

By craving it so much, your body and astral body are more likely to project. This means you can use it with other techniques like the rope technique without too many problems.

Also, bear in mind that you shouldn't completely deprive yourself of water for more than a few hours. This is best done from the hours of about 6-7PM until when you go to bed. Or, if you wake up in the early hours of the morning, just don't have a drink but instead eat some salt.

If you feel faint or feel like you really need a drink at any point, drink. Just try again the next day, because dehydration is not fun and not a joke.

10: The Stretch Out Technique

As with the other techniques, lying down in a relaxed state is necessary. Try to imagine you feet becoming longer by about an inch. Once you have this visualized this, let your feet go back to normal. Repeat this exercise with your head.

Then alternate between your head and your feet extending the distance until you can stretch them out by two feet or so.

Dizziness is quite possible and at some point the vibrational stage should begin and you will eventually float toward the ceiling.

This is more of just a way of getting into the vibrational stage faster. As we explained before, the vibrational stage is where you'll feel vibrations, sounds and might even see shapes and colors as you rise out of your body slowly. It can last for a few seconds or a few minutes.

So with the stretch out technique you need to keep your focus on the vibrational stage. This is what you're aiming to do, so make sure to focus on that and nothing else.

11: Finding objects or information

Try and find an object in your room next time you try to astral travel.

Pick a readily identifiable object to describe and remember. When you get back to physical reality, find the object again and see if you were right. Obviously, it works best if you pick objects that you wouldn't have known were there.

Try working with objects in another room that someone else has placed for you to find. Another fun exercise is to get someone to write down some information in another room. Then project into that room and read it as a test of your skills.

This is similar to remote viewing, although you're not going to be awake in your physical body when you do this. The sensations will be very similar though, so give it a try!

It works better with smaller and more obvious details and objects, things that you can instantly recognise if you were to see them, think about them or hear about them. I like to try this with small things like totems or dice etc.

12: The lucid dreaming method

This is going to be a way of using a lucid dream to move into an astral projection experience. This won't work for everyone, and actually this is quite a difficult technique.

It's difficult because it requires you to be able to actually lucid dream first. If you can't lucid dream, there are many articles and sites showing you how to do that online, just do a google search and have a read.

So once you're lucid, make sure to prolong the lucid dream by spinning around and you're then going to ask the DREAM itself to help you become astral.

Shout out loud to the dream while you're lucid 'make me astral project'. Simple, right?

You'll find the dream itself (which is your own subconscious mind) will help you do this. Not only will it help you, but the more often you ask the dream for things like this, the more likely it is it will randomly help you.

So, after you've asked the dream to make you astral project, you'll find that your dream starts to collapse.

The dream scene around you can fade and go to black, and you'll find yourself in an aware state but with your eyes closed.

From here, try and gently open your eyes but NOT your physical eyes. Remember how we spoke about visualising your astral body and astral hand for the rope technique?

The same thing applies here.

All you're going to do is visualise opening your astral eyes and moving around your ASTRAL world with that body. Don't think about your physical body, and if you feel like you're going to accidental open your REAL eyes, stop yourself and don't move (then try again in a few minutes).

If you open your real eyes, you'll wake yourself up too much and end up just not being able to do it until the next night or morning. And that would be very annoying, so try and stay focused here.

13: The Self-Visualization Method

Like the Point Shift method, this is one of the more difficult techniques to master. This method requires envisioning a detailed clone of yourself, and it works best from an environment that is very familiar to you.

When you begin the visualization, begin at your feet and move your way up throughout your body. Take the time to envision details that will make the body double feel more real.

At this point, attempt to allow your body-double to stand up or sit up.

You may start to feel a pressure in your head or in your chest. Don't panic, this is the projection point kicking in. If all goes to plan, your awareness will now have shifted entirely to the projected body.

When you do this, it's important to realise that your thoughts will wander. When doing any visualisation technique your thoughts can be your biggest enemy. By closing your eyes and focusing on thinking about something visual, it can be very easy to get distracted.

The ONE biggest thing that'll help you overcome that problem, is meditation even single morning.

Meditation has been with me fore most of my life, and it's helped in more ways than one. By meditating every single morning, you'll be much more easily able to focus on one thing for a long period of time. That's a crucial skill for lucid dreams and astral projectors alike.

A really effective spinoff of this little technique is this:

Lay down on your back and close your eyes. Do this at the same time you would have done the other techniques, in the early hours of the morning. Spend a few minutes relaxing your muscles and mind, and then do this:

Imagine a detailed image of YOURSELf laying in the bed. Start by visualising yourself from about 6 feet away from the bed, and just let the image form in your mind.

Don't move any of your muscles of limbs, and just let the image sort of 'create itself' as you float there. Don't try and force anything, and don't create the image. Just imagine what you would see if you were floating 6 feet away from your bed.

Let the image of yourself form on the bed, and just observe it. Look at the details, see your hair on the pillow, the covers wrapped around you and the wall behind the bed.

See it all, and just watch.

After a few minutes, you'll realise that actually the image sort of moves around on its own. Maybe you can notice yourself breathing on the bed, or you see yourself move slightly but in a way that you didn't imagine or intend to happen.

At that moment, remember not to panic.

You're now astral projecting. While you thought you were forming the image of yourself on the bed, you were REALLY forming your astral body 6 feet away from the bed.

It's a very clever mind hack and a way of getting your attention to go away from your physical body. Doing this lets your astral body form very easily, and without hardly any effort at all. But I warn you this one can freak you out if you're not used to it!

14: The Rolling-Out Technique for Projection

This is not a complete method for astral projection but more of a supplemental resource for when projection has not quite been successful.

Its helpful to alternate this technique with others when projection is not going well, or use it to finish the projection after using the rope technique.

This is a method of inducing an astral projection while in bed or in a reclining position. It is effective because the act of rolling in bed is something is commonly experienced many times a night, and the familiarity of it makes it easy to imagine for the purpose of helping to induce a projection.

Feel yourself rolling back and forth in your bed, and allow your imagined viewpoint to reflect each new position.

This technique for astral projection is usually enough to trigger a successful projection, even when you have found yourself unsuccessful at other methods.

It sounds simple, because it is, and it's really more of an addition to the other techniques but it's very effective! You can combine this with most other techniques.

Hopefully by now you've got a bit more of an idea of the sort of feeling you're aiming for, and how it would look or feel.

It's a subtle shifting of your awareness and sensations from the physical to the astral, and it can happen fast if you do it right. It can be an instant thing, or it can take up to an hour, it really depends on which technique you're using and how you're doing it.

15: The Kick System

You may have noticed, while driving you can easily find yourself in a trance, and then you snap out of it wondering how you got where you did.

We can often lose track of time, or travel somewhere without really remembering much of the process of getting there.

You might be able to remember a time when you were driving or on a plane but feeling very tired. You lean back for just a few seconds and close your eyes, but then you're SNAPPED back to being awake by a movement by your head facing down or to the side?

That's the feeling you're going to be aiming for here.

But you're not trying to HAVE the feeling, you're trying to REMEMBER the feeling. It works best with the feeling you get on a plane when you've not had any sleep, and you can't sleep because the plane seats are too small and uncomfortable.

It's possible to use our remembered experiences to help induce astral travel, by recollecting the feeling of motion combined with the moving landscape.

Sort of like the 'Kick' in the movie Inception, you're going to be inducing that feeling by remembering memories of it. When you remember the feeling, try and imagine it was happening NOW, as you lay there in bed.

But instead of imagining the feeling resulting in you waking up and looking around the plane, imagine you're going to be floating above your body.

Again, this works really well when you're already really tired, like in the early hours of the morning. You can actually use this technique ON a plane in exactly the same way! The idea is you're targeting that sensation of being thrown from one state of consciousness to another.

This should result in a deep trance, allowing the projector to now switch to another method to make the actual projection. When you get this one right, it happens really fast, and you'll be instantly astral projecting floating around your room.

16: The Picture Technique

Really "feeling" and "seeing" the details around you is the key for making this astral projection technique successful.

Start by allowing an imaginary viewpoint to get closer and closer to the image, and then gently but firmly push your consciousness into the picture. This technique allows the Astral Traveler to explore a virtual world or worlds, and also use this as a starting point for traveling to other astral worlds

One problem that people often find with astral projection is that they can successfully project to a specific place or astral realm, but shortly find the destination morphing into something different.

The Picture Technique for astral travel avoids these kinds of problems, transporting the traveler to a much more vivid world that could be explored many times and the results of each journey are much more likely to be consistent.

17: The "Stay awake" method

This method requires going to bed when tired and keeping your eyes open as much as possible.

Stay as relaxed as possible and take in the room taking care to look at all the details until it is imprinted in your mind. Do this until you fall asleep and the astral process begins.

What's interesting about this, is that it's essentially the same as the WILD method for lucid dreaming except you keep your eyes open. WILD is a wake induced lucid dream, and the technique involves the same things.

You lay down, close your eyes and then simply don't move. You let sleep paralysis set in, and keep your MIND awake while your BODY falls asleep.

It's a beautiful technique because when you learn it, you can technically do it ay night any time. It just involves staying awake while your body falls asleep. The downsides to this are that if you can't fall asleep, it can feel like torture trying to keep your mind awake!

Also if you do this first thing at night, you'll find it hard to actually fall asleep and you'll end up just staring at your ceiling for several hours without really doing anything.

This works best in the early hours of the morning during the OBE sweet spots we mentioned.

Tips and tricks

Tips and Tricks for Success

That is a lot of techniques to take in and master straight off the bat, so take your time. Practice one at a time, and don't stress out about it. Here are some tips and tricks for astral projecting that will help you and make things a bit easier for you.

1: Motivation

The most important ingredient for any successful projection is motivation.

Without this, there will not be enough enthusiasm to succeed. It is important to keep the preparation time brief, so it is not exhausting. One thing a new projector usually has is an abundance of enthusiasm.

Try and keep this up and make sure to inspire and motivate yourself every day to keep going. Watch films that inspire you to do it, or think about it and read stories of people that have done it!

2: Chakras

As a preparation process for astral protection, work on developing your chakras; learn about them and meditate visualizing each one being healthy and in balance.

There's far too much detail about chakras to go into in this ebook but you can learn a lot just by researching chakras and how they work. In general, try and meditate, drink only filtered water and eat a vegan or plant based diet.

Those things alone will cleanse and strengthen most of your chakras and make sure your body and mind are functioning at very high vibrations.

3: Light

You cannot perform astral projection with bright lights; darken your room, but still keep it from being totally dark. You can use a blackout curtain or shades to do this, or you could get a sleep mask and use that.

The easiest thing to do is to remove any artificial sources of light like LED lights from chargers and things like that. Those things can be put into another room. The only light you should really use when astral projecting, is a dim candle or two in the corners of the room.

4: Crystals

It can be helpful to use a quartz crystal to raise your vibrations while attempting to project. Hold the crystal on the third eye above your eyebrows with closed eyes. Feel the vibrations and envision you can envision different colors of light. The crystal will protect you through vibrations.

5: Sounds

Binaural beats encourage your brain to synchronize at a set frequency. Resources are all over the internet and can be obtained for free. Just get a pair of headphones and listen to the beats as you attempt to project, The best results for achieving projection have been experienced at a binaural beat of around 4htz.

6: Wear Loose Fitting Clothing

Dress appropriately in loose-fitting and comfortable clothes. It is also perfectly acceptable to wear nothing at all. This is a really important one actually.

Most people try and astral project wearing normal trousers and shirts. These are often restrictive and uncomfortable. Wear something like harem pants or a night gown that won't restrict your movement or blood flow in any way.

7: Adjust the Temperature

During astral travel, the temperature of your body drops slightly just as your physical body falls asleep. It might be a good idea to put a sheet or blanket over yourself and make up for the temperature drop. You could also raise the temperature of the room slightly as well.

8: Turn off your phone and electronic devices

Create a quiet and relaxing atmosphere. Turn off all electrical devices that may distract you. Make sure to turn off your mobile phone too or put it in silent mode to avoid distractions.

In fact, most devices like phones and laptops should NOT be kept in the same room as where you sleep. They make your sleep quality worse, and lessen the chances of being able to astral project successfully.

9: Self suggestions

Use this with any astral projection method of your choice, and say to yourself over and over "When I fall asleep, I will be able to project astrally. The power of suggestion and repetition is useful and should be used frequently.

You can also write on notes to put around the house things like 'I will astral project tonight' or 'I can astral project easily'. Every time you see these notes it will make the beliefs that little bit stronger, and you'll be more likely to actually do it.

10: Wish Fulfilment

Understand that astral plane fulfils fantasies — everything you wish may become your reality while you are there, so wish wisely.

Often we think we want certain things, when we really want other things. Take a few moments to think about why you're learning to astral project, and what it's going to do for you.

If you're solely learning to cause damage to someone or to spy on someone, there's not much chance of you being able to do that. Astral projection is a high vibration activity and requires your soul and intention to be pure and honest.

Sure, you can learn to use it for bad things but it's much harder, and not needed. Be a good person and don't use astral projection for bad things!

11: Commands

Use strong mental commands when you want to do something in the astral plane. For example, "Go to China! Now!" Soon you will be there. You can travel everywhere—to different galaxies, etc. Your power of desire may create new worlds and environments.

This works the same as it does in lucid dreams. The things you expect to happen usually will happen. But remember that in the astral realm, it's outside of your mind so things are not ALWAYS in your control.

You're nowhere near as in control as you can be in lucid dreams, so be careful. You can still give the astral realm commands and it usually helps you out.

12: Astral Guides

After a while, your astral guide (or guides) will make themselves known. Show gratitude to your guide and obey his or her recommendations and teachings. You can find them faster by simply searching for them.

A common thing you can do (which also works in lucid dreams) is just shouting out 'where's my dream guide?'. Your dream guide will literally appear in front of yo most times, and make themselves known.

The dream guides want to be found and used, it's their divine purpose. Use it to your advantage and look for them. You can find them in most places in the astral realm, and they'll usually find you when they think you're ready as well.

13: Keep a Journal

You may be surprised to know that many people who think that they cannot project astrally, simply have difficulty remembering their experiences.

Because of the nature of the astral projection, not being able to remember the experience might make it feel as though it didn't take place.

This is actually really important:

Your memory functions differently in the astral world. It's not the same as just having a dream and then waking up and remembering that dream.

It involves sending the memories back to the physical world, and it can take a lot of practice to actually be able to remember your experiences in detail. This is the EXACT reason why it's very difficult to 'go into the future and predict the lottery' with astral projection.

It's because things like the lottery are firstly very random, and when you astral travel to the future it's more a potential future than the EXACT indisputable future, so it never really works.

But the most annoying problem is that of your memory.

The best way of improving this is to simply keep a journal by your bed along with a pen. Write your experiences down and make sure you look back at them the next night as well.

What is the best time to project?

Many people try to project at night but this is actually a mistake.

After a long day, the mind and body are tired, and most often the astral attempt ends in sleep without projection.

Most say that the early morning hours are the best time for projection, especially right after waking up. This is the hypnagogic state. From this relaxed state, it is easier to fall back asleep but staying awake in the mind.

Another reason to try astral projection in the morning, is because melatonin levels are high during these hours and you've had a chance to deal with what was on your mind from the day before.

During this time cortisol levels are starting to build which makes for a more alert mental state. Brainwave frequencies, or theta waves, are in a desirable range of 4-8 hz.

This is the absolute perfect time for lucid dreaming and OBEs like astral projection. Use it wisely and don't destroy your sleep with things like coffee, nicotine, bright lights and alcohol. These things lower your vibrations and make it harder to astral project.

Wake up, Get up, and go back to bed tip

Set your alarm for an earlier time. After you wake up, spend some time doing other activities to make yourself fully awake.

Reading about astral projection is strongly recommended because it helps prepare the mind subconsciously for astral projection.

After 30-60 minutes have passed, return to your place where you do astral projection and many report that this process aids in getting to the state of mind needed to project.

How is the pineal gland linked?

The pineal gland has been a topic of fascination throughout history.

Also called the third eye, there are plenty of references to the pineal gland throughout literature and history. The pineal gland is shaped like a pine cone and is approximately the size of a pea.

It is located in the central part of the brain between the left and right hemispheres of the brain.

It's been referred to as the 'god organ' and thought to be the link between this world and the spiritual or higher world. All we know right now is that it's a VERY important part of our bodies, and it's essential that we don't allow it to become inactive due to chemicals we ingest.

The pineal gland can be seen in some x-rays due to calcification that is a result of fluoride. Fluoride is typically found in unfiltered water and toothpaste and when the calcium builds up, it causes it to harden.

Calcium affects the pineal gland more than it affects teeth or bone. It is part of the endocrine system in the body and it is responsible for the release of hormones. The pineal gland releases melatonin which regulates sleep and wake patterns, mood and growth.

Many schools and mystical traditions have known this area of the brain to be the connecting link between both the physical world that we have come to know as our own, as well as the spiritual world beyond time.

The pineal gland is considered the most important part of our bodies in initiating supernatural powers as well as the highest source of ethereal energy. Psychic talents have been associated with the wakening of this organ.

Because the pineal gland is located so deep and protected in the brain, some believe that there is an importance of this gland, so important that it has been linked to mysteries and mysticism.

Activation of the Pineal Gland

The pineal gland is activated by light among other things.

Many people have reported feeling a pressure at the base of the brain after having their pineal gland awakened and opened. This pressure can be experienced when one connects to a higher frequency.

It is said that when the pineal gland or 'third eye' is awakened, one is able to see beyond space time, into time space. It raises the frequency on which one operates and moves one into a higher consciousness.

All forms of out-of-body travel are connected with the third eye.

This includes meditation, visualization, and yoga. Once the third eye is awakened, you will be able to see beyond the physical world.

As one practices opening the 'third eye', it will come more naturally to you if you practice frequently. Dream messages and supernatural abilities will increase. Many begin practicing with their eyes closed but in time and with much practice, one will be able to see into the spiritual world of time space with their physical eyes open.

When the pineal gland is activated, it becomes the line of communication with the spiritual world and those beyond it. The crown chakra moves down towards the pineal gland in a vortex.

When the vortex touches the pineal gland, pure energy is received. This pure energy is also called Prana or life force. The more one practices, the higher the vibrations in the body raise and the astral body will then be able to separate from the physical body.

After meditation and after the body has completely let go of worldly needs, one can try to activate the pineal gland through meditation by staring at the point in the middle of the forehead.

One must first start to feel a withdrawal from the senses as well as a withdrawal from the ego. Visualize your physical body escaping through a door in the brain.

People who have had near death experiences have reported experiencing astral projection. Many report hearing a "popping" sound when the astral body separates from the physical body.

Visualization is the first step in directing the energy of the body to activate the pineal gland. Once the magnetic field is created, it surrounds the pineal gland. The creative imagination visualizes something and the thought energy of the mind gives it life and direction.

Developing the third eye is very important if you wish to succeed in projection. Intuition can also improve with third eye development. When the third eye begins to activate, flashes of memory and knowledge of the astral plane will start to occur.

This will become more and more frequent as the third eye develops. When reaching certain frequencies, the ego begins to shrink. This is the 'theta' state which means we are still conscious yet in a deeply restful state.

Final thoughts

Final thoughts

We made it!

A 1992 Gallup Poll suggested up to 5% of people have experienced some form of projection in their lives. (Now imagine if that percentage were much closer to 100%.)

That's a huge percentage, when you consider that other HUGE movements and trends are the same sort of percentage of the population, or lower.

Some people use it for spiritual advancement while others use it to develop their intuition and gain clarity about their life purpose. Imagine what our world could be like if we all explored this realm!

The possibilities are endless!

Traveling to other worlds where normals laws of time and space do not exist can open up a whole new perspective on life. Learning to practice astral travel will give you access to knowledge and wisdom that you would never have access to without it.

Hopefully you've enjoyed this beginners guide to astral projection and feel ready to get started. The best way of practicing this is to take a few minutes every day and practice ONE of TWO of the techniques mentioned here.

Meditate every morning, eat right and sleep enough.

Results will come within a few days/weeks, but you must put in the effort, otherwise you won't experience astral projection. Too many people go online and buy ebooks hoping that by just reading them, they'll experience the results.

Of course you CAN, but you need to put in the efforts, and actually practice the things you've learned. You're in for a hell of a ride, so buckle up, and safe travels!

Bonuses and resources

I've found a few things that might help you out with this, which can make astral projection more likely.

Astral projection MASTERY: Our much more detailed astral projection course complete with several custom binaural beats audio tracks and more. Very valuable and effective course for diving DEEPER once you've learned how to astral project.

To learn more about Astral projection MASTERY type this URL into your browser:

AstralHQ.com/Mastery

And as a thank you for completing this ebook, you can get a MASSIVE discount on the mastery course by entering this code at the checkout: 'ENDOFBOOKBONUS'

That's it for now guys.
Good luck!

Copyright AstralHQ.com 2019; all rights reserved. You do not have permission to resell, reproduce, or otherwise distribute this ebook.

www.ingramcontent.com/pod-product-compliance
Lightning Source LLC
LaVergne TN
LVHW021129050225
803024LV00007B/302